On the Go
Tractors in Action

David and Penny Glover

PowerKiDS
press.
New York

Published in 2008 by The Rosen Publishing Group, Inc.
29 East 21st Street, New York, NY 10010

First Edition

Editor: Camilla Lloyd
Editorial Assistant: Katie Powell
Designer: Elaine Wilkinson
Picture Researcher: Diana Morris

Picture Credits:
The author and publisher would like to thank the following for allowing these
pictures to be reproduced in this publication:
John Deere: Cover, 1, 4, 5, 7, 9, 11, 12, 13, 16b, 17, 18; Humphrey Evans/Sylvia
Cordaiy PL/Alamy: 14, Glyn Thomas/Alamy: 15t, All Over Photography/Alamy:
15b, Greenshoots Communications/Alamy: 16t, Bartomeu Amengual/Alamy:
19, Dennis Macdonald/Alamy: 20, 21; Nick Wheeler/Corbis: 22, Paul
Souders/Corbis: 10b; Holt Studios/FLPA Images: 8, 10t; Chris Saltberger/Image
Bank/Getty Images: 6.
With special thanks to John Deere.

Library of Congress Cataloging-in-Publication Data

Glover, David, 1953 Sept. 4-
    Tractors in action / David and Penny Glover. — 1st ed.
        p. cm. — (On the go)
    Includes index.
    ISBN 978-1-4042-4309-5 (library binding)
    1. Tractors—Juvenile literature. I. Glover, Penny. II. Title. III. Series.

TL233.15.G583 2006
629.225'2—dc22

                                    2007032271

Manufactured in China

Contents

What are tractors?

Tractors are vehicles that move things. Most tractors work on farms. They pull **plows** and other farm machines. A farmer can hook a **trailer** to the tractor to pull a heavy **load**.

tractor

trailer

Some tractors can lift and push, as well as pull. This tractor is lifting straw.

lifting arm

Tractor quiz
Where do most tractors work?

Tractor parts

The tractor driver sits in the **cab**. This is high up so he can see all around. The tractor's **engine** is at the front, under the **hood**.

cab

hood

hitch

wheels

The tractor's **hitch** is at the back. This is where the tractor hooks onto the things it pulls.

This tractor has a **scoop** to lift sand and soil.

scoop

spotlights

When it gets dark, the driver can turn on **spotlights** so he or she can see to work.

Tractor quiz
What is under the tractor's hood?

In the cab

control switches

steering wheel

The driver turns the front wheels to the right or left with the steering wheel. This makes the tractor turn.

Levers, switches, and buttons work the tractor parts.

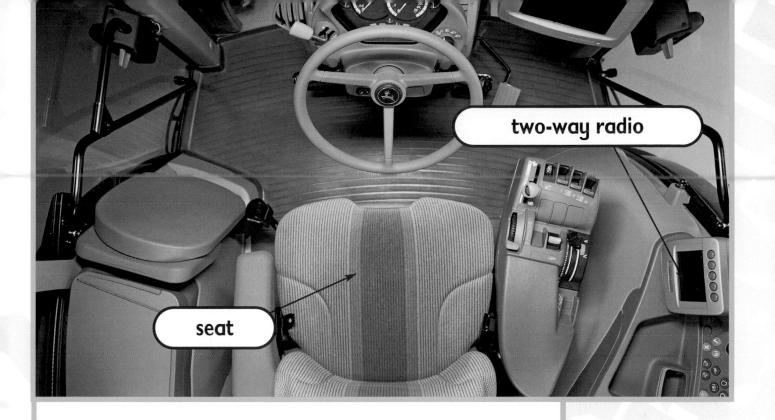

two-way radio

seat

The driver's seat is comfortable.
The driver sometimes sits in the
tractor all day to plow a field.
The driver can talk to other people
with a **two-way radio**.

Tractor quiz

How can a tractor driver
talk to other people
while he or she works?

Tractor wheels

The tractor has big wheels, so it can cross soft mud and rough ground. Small wheels would sink or get stuck. A rod called an **axle** attaches each wheel to the tractor.

axle

tread

Tractor wheels have thick rubber tires to grip the ground. The tires have deep **treads**, so they don't slip. This works like the treads on the bottom of a pair of gym shoes.

Tractor quiz
What are tractor tires made from?

What makes it go?

engine

The tractor's engine makes it go.
It turns the wheels to move the
tractor forward.

The engine runs on **diesel fuel**.
The driver fills the fuel tank from
a tank in the farmyard.

The tractor's engine also powers the different machines the tractor pulls. This tractor is pulling a grass cutter.

grass cutter

Tractor quiz
What fuel does a tractor engine run on?

Tractors at work

blade

plow

When there is a field to plow, the farmer hitches the plow to the tractor. The tractor pulls the plow across the field.

The plow breaks up the soil. Then the farmer can plant the seeds.

Tractor quiz
What does a plow do?

fertilizer spreader

If there is a trailer to pull, or fertilizer to spread, a tractor can do that, too.

Tractor to the rescue! When another vehicle gets stuck in the mud or breaks down, a tractor can pull it.

Special jobs

lifeboat

Some tractors do jobs away from the farm. This tractor pulls a lifeboat and its crew in and out of the water.

This tractor lifts logs in the forest.

This mini-tractor is cutting the grass in a garden.

Tractor quiz
What might a tractor lift in the forest?

Old-fashioned tractors did not have a cab. If the tractor rolled over, the driver could be trapped underneath.

safety cab

flashing light

Tractors are slower than cars. When a tractor drives along a road, a flashing light warns car drivers it is there.

Tractor quiz
Why were old tractors dangerous?

Tractor fun

Sometimes tractors take part in pulling contests. It's a tractor tug of war! Special tractors with powerful engines compete to pull the heaviest load.

Children can
ride tractors, too.
This tractor is
pedal-powered.
It does not have
an engine.

Tractor quiz

**What do the tractors do
in a pulling contest?**

Old tractors

Before tractors were invented, horses pulled plows.

The first tractors were powered by steam. They were called **traction engines**. Then the diesel engine was invented.

Tractor words

axle
The rod through the middle of a wheel.

cab
The part of the tractor where the driver sits.

diesel
The fuel a tractor engine uses to make it go.

engine
The part of the tractor that makes it move.

fuel
Something that burns inside an engine to make it work.

hitch
The part that hooks the tractor to a trailer, a plow, or other farm machines.

hood
The engine cover.

load
Something you lift or carry.

plow
The farm machine a tractor pulls to break up the soil.

scoop
The big bucket for scooping up sand or soil.

spotlights
The lights on the cab of the tractor that let the driver see when it is dark.

traction engine
The name of the first steam-powered tractors.

trailer
The part that is hooked onto the tractor to carry the load.

tread
Deep grooves on the tractor's tires that grip soft ground.

two-way radio
The radio in a tractor that lets the driver talk to other people.

Quiz answers

Page 5 On farms.

Page 7 The engine.

Page 9 With a two-way radio.

Page 11 Rubber.

Page13 Diesel fuel.

Page 14 It breaks up the soil.

Page 17 Logs.

Page 19 Because they did not have a cab to

keep the driver safe.

Page 21 They compete to pull the heaviest load.

Index

Web Sites
Due to the changing nature of Internet links, PowerKids Press has developed an online list of Web sites related to the subject of this book. This site is regularly updated. Please use this link to access this list:
www.powerkidslinks.com/otg/tract